WHAT I KNOW ABOUT GOD

Carol Lynn Pearson

Gibbs Smith

First Edition
29 28 27 26 25 5 4 3 2 1

Published by
Gibbs Smith
570 N. Sportsplex Dr.
Kaysville, Utah 84037

1.800.835.4993 orders
www.gibbs-smith.com

Designed by Sheryl Dickert

Printed and bound in China

This product is made of FSC®-certified and other controlled material.

MIX
Paper | Supporting responsible forestry
FSC® C153458

Library of Congress Control Number: 2024941761

ISBN: 978-1-4236-6840-4

INTRODUCTION

The word "God" has been so hijacked and abused as to make it unattractive to many people. And the "ownership" of God is surely one of the most distressing ills of our time.

What I Know About God assists in reclaiming the Creator for everyone, reminding us of the Mystery, the Mythic, the Poetic by presenting 125 quotes from the best minds throughout history.

Carl Jung, Shakespeare, Voltaire, R. Buckminster Fuller, Walt Whitman, Emily Dickinson, Ralph Waldo Emerson, Van Gogh, and many others—including representatives of all the major religions—share remarkable insights that create a conversation about the Divine that is both inviting and uniting.

This is a book to be opened when a child asks, "What is God?" or when any one of us asks on a dark day or any other day, "Where is God?"

How can we live in harmony?

First we need to know we are all madly in love with the same God.

—SAINT THOMAS AQUINAS

The very word "God" suggests care, kindness, goodness. We give God the name of good: it is only by shortening it that it becomes God.

—HENRY WARD BEECHER

TO LOVE ANOTHER PERSON IS TO SEE THE FACE OF GOD.

—VICTOR HUGO

How important the concept of God is, and how instead of valuing what has been given us, we with light hearts spurn it because of absurdities that have been attached to it.

—LEO TOLSTOY

I could not say I believe.

I KNOW!

I have had the experience of being gripped

by something that is stronger than myself,

something that people call God.

—CARL JUNG

WHEN WE LOSE GOD, IT IS NOT GOD WHO IS LOST.

—UNKNOWN

God is a verb, not a noun

proper or improper.

—R. BUCKMINSTER FULLER

I cannot imagine how the clockwork of the universe can exist without a clockmaker.

—VOLTAIRE

For, after all, put it as we may to ourselves, we are all of us from birth to death guests at a table which we did not spread. The sun, the earth, love, friends, our very breath are parts of the banquet. . . . Shall we think of the day as a chance to come nearer to our Host, and to find out something of Him who has fed us so long?

—REBECCA HARDING DAVIS

For light I go directly to the Source of light,

not to any of the reflections.

—PEACE PILGRIM

THERE IS A GOD-SHAPED VACUUM IN THE HEART OF EACH MAN.

—BLAISE PASCAL

“What do you think of God,” the teacher asked.

After a pause, the young pupil replied,

“He’s not a think, he’s a feel.”

—PAUL FROST

Life is God's novel. Let Him write it.

—ISAAC BASHEVIS SINGER

All are but parts of one stupendous whole,

Whose body Nature is, and God the soul.

—ALEXANDER POPE

In nature we see where God has been. In our fellow man, we see where He is still at work.

—ROBERT BREAULT

Whenever I see sunbeams coming through clouds, it always looks to me like God shining Himself down onto us. The thing about sunbeams is they're always there even though we can't always see them. Same with God.

—ADELINE CULLEN RAY

GOD IS THE PERFECT POET.

—ROBERT BROWNING

God enters by a private door into each individual.

—RALPH WALDO EMERSON

If you don’t know what’s meant by God, watch a forsythia branch or a lettuce leaf sprout.

—MARTIN H. FISCHER

People see God every day,

they just don't recognize Him.

—PEARL BAILEY

But I cannot help thinking that the best way to know God is to love many things.

—VINCENT VAN GOGH

The feeling remains that God is on the journey, too.

—SAINT TERESA OF AVILA

A man can no more diminish God's glory by refusing to worship Him than a lunatic can put out the sun by scribbling the word "darkness" on the walls of his cell.

—C. S. LEWIS

The soul can split the sky in two and let the face of God shine through.

—EDNA ST. VINCENT MILLAY

We need to find God, and He cannot be found in noise and restlessness.

GOD IS THE FRIEND OF SILENCE.

See how nature—trees, flowers, grass—grows in silence; see the stars, the moon, and the sun, how they move in silence.

—MOTHER TERESA

You can tell the size of your God by looking at the size of your worry list. The longer your list, the smaller your God.

—UNKNOWN

If God had wanted to be a
big secret, He would not have
created babbling brooks and
whispering pines.

—ROBERT BREAULT

Don’t look for God where He is needed most; if you didn’t bring Him there, He isn’t there.

—MIGNON MCLAUGHLIN

"I was six when I saw that everything was God, and my hair stood up, and all," Teddy said. "It was on a Sunday, I remember. My sister was a tiny child then, and she was drinking her milk, and all of a sudden I saw that she was God and the milk was God. I mean, all she was doing was pouring God into God, if you know what I mean."

—J. D. SALINGER

Man is born broken.

He lives by mending.

The grace of God is glue.

—EUGENE O'NEILL

BEFORE ME, EVEN AS BEHIND, GOD IS, AND ALL IS WELL.

—JOHN GREENLEAF WHITTIER

The function of prayer is not to influence God, but rather to change the nature of the one who prays.

—SOREN KIERKEGAARD

What comes into our minds when we think about God is the most important thing about us.

—A. W. TOZER

We turn to God for help when our foundations are shaking, only to learn that it is God who is shaking them.

—C. WEST CHURCHMAN

GOD SAID,

"I was a hidden treasure.

I would fain be known.

So I created Man."

—PROPHET MUHAMMAD

God will hold us responsible for all the wonderful things that we have refused to enjoy.

—PROVERB

God must love the common man—

He made so many of them.

—ATTRIBUTED TO ABRAHAM LINCOLN

I GAVE IN AND ADMITTED THAT GOD WAS GOD.

—C. S. LEWIS

There are people in the world so hungry, that God cannot appear to them except in the form of bread.

—MAHATMA GANDHI

God is really only another artist. He invented the giraffe, the elephant, and the cat. He has no real style, He just goes on trying other things.

—PABLO PICASSO

The end of life is to be like God, and the soul following God will be like Him.

—SOCRATES

Never lose an opportunity of seeing anything beautiful, for beauty is God's handwriting.

—RALPH WALDO EMERSON

God is a metaphor for that which transcends all levels of intellectual thought. It's as simple as that.

—JOSEPH CAMPBELL

Every person is a God in embryo.

Its only desire is to be born.

—DEEPAK CHOPRA

If God did not exist, it would be necessary to invent Him.

—VOLTAIRE

God loves each of us as if there were only one of us.

—SAINT AUGUSTINE

God has entrusted me with myself.

—EPICTETUS

Back of the loaf is the snowy flour,

And back of the flour the mill;

And back of the mill is the wheat, and the shower,

And the sun, and the Father's will.

—MALTBIE D. BABCOCK

THERE IS NO DOOR IN MY THEATRE THROUGH WHICH GOD CANNOT SEE.

—EDWIN BOOTH

Earth's crammed with heaven,

And every common bush afire with God.

But only he who sees takes off his shoes,

The rest sit round and pluck blackberries.

—ELIZABETH BARRETT BROWNING

God! Sing, ye meadow-streams, with gladsome voice!
Ye pine-groves, with your soft and soul-like sounds! . . .
Earth with her thousand voices, praises God.

—SAMUEL TAYLOR COLERIDGE

God moves in a mysterious way
His wonders to perform;
He plants His footsteps in the sea
And rides upon the storm.

—WILLIAM COWPER

TO BE IS TO LIVE WITH GOD.

—RALPH WALDO EMERSON

Here lies the body of John Smith, who for forty years cobbled shoes in this village to the glory of God.

—EPITAPH

GOD GAVE YOU A GIFT OF 86,400 SECONDS TODAY. HAVE YOU USED ONE TO SAY "THANK YOU?"

—WILLIAM ARTHUR WARD

This is well-nigh the greatest of discoveries a man can make, that God is not confined in churches, but that the streets are sacred because His presence is there.

—R. C. GILLIE

Why are you so anxious

to see God with your eyes closed?

See Him with your eyes open—

in the form of the poor, the starved,

the illiterate, and the afflicted.

—HINDU TO A CHRISTIAN

God loves an idle rainbow

No less than laboring seas.

—RALPH HODGSON

The world is charged with the grandeur of God.

—GERARD MANLEY HOPKINS

Call on God,

but row away from the rocks.

—INDIAN PROVERB

Our Father dwells in tents as well as in the temples, but His favorite abiding-place is in the hearts of mankind.

—J. FRED JONES

I am a little pencil in the hand of a writing God
who is sending a love letter to the world.

—MOTHER TERESA

We know God easily,

if we do not constrain

ourselves to define Him.

—JOSEPH JOUBERT

If the blind put their hand in God's, they find their way more surely than those who see but have not faith or purpose.

—HELEN KELLER

WHO THOU ART I KNOW NOT,

BUT THIS MUCH I KNOW:

THOU HAS SET THE PLEIADES

IN A SILVER ROW.

—HARRY KEMP

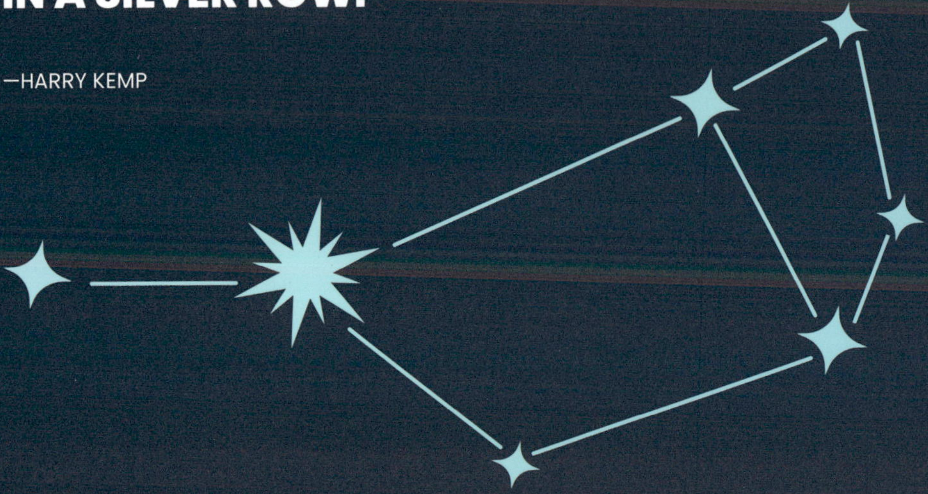

"How do you know," a Bedouin asked, "that there is a God?" "In the same way," he replied, "that I know, on looking at the sand, when a man or beast has crossed the desert—by His footprints in the world around me."

—HENRY PARRY LIDDON

Is there any other seat of the Divinity than the earth, sea, air, and heavens, and virtuous minds? Why do we seek God elsewhere? He is whatever you see; He is wherever you move.

—LUCAN

GOD DOESN'T ALWAYS SMOOTH THE PATH, BUT SOMETIMES HE PUTS SPRINGS IN THE WAGON.

—MARSHALL LUCAS

How often we look upon God as our last and feeblest resource!

We go to Him because we have nowhere else to go.

And then we learn that the storms of life have driven us,

not upon the rocks, but into the desired haven.

—GEORGE MACDONALD

God, I can push the grass apart

And lay my finger on Thy heart!

—EDNA ST. VINCENT MILLAY

God is love, and he that dwelleth in love dwelleth in God, and God in him.

—1 JOHN 4:16

The heavens declare

the glory of God; and

the firmament showeth

His handywork.

—PSALM 19:1

There is a God within us, and

we glow when He stirs us.

—OVID

THE WORLD IS GOD'S EPISTLE TO MANKIND—HIS THOUGHTS ARE FLASHING UPON US FROM EVERY DIRECTION.

—PLATO

God often visits us,

but most of the time

we are not at home.

—PHILIBERT JOSEPH ROUX

**God shall be
my hope, my stay,
my guide, and
lantern to my feet.**

—WILLIAM SHAKESPEARE

MANY MILLIONS SEARCH FOR GOD AND FIND HIM IN THEIR HEARTS.

—SIKH PROVERB

I used to ask God to help me.

Then I asked if I might help Him.

I ended up by asking to do His

work through me.

—HUDSON TAYLOR

It is a great mistake to suppose that God is only, or even chiefly, concerned with religion.

—WILLIAM TEMPLE, ARCHBISHOP OF CANTERBURY

In the faces of men and women I see God,
and in my own face in the glass;
I find letters from God dropped in the street,
and every one is signed by God's name.

—WALT WHITMAN

I SHALL ALWAYS BE MORE CERTAIN *THAT* GOD IS THAN *WHAT* HE IS.

—WILLIAM E. HOCKING

If we cannot find God in your house or in mine, upon the roadside or the margin of the sea . . . I do not think we should discern Him any more on the grass of Eden, or beneath the moonlight of Gethsemane.

—JAMES MARTINEAU

Only if God is revealed in the history of the Syrians and Philistines can He be revealed in the history of Israel. Only if He chooses all men for His own can He choose any at all.

—WILLIAM TEMPLE, ARCHBISHOP OF CANTERBURY

He does not prove the existence of God; being is God!

—JOHANN WOLFGANG VON GOETHE

Whilst everything around me is ever-changing, ever-dying, there is underlying all that change a living power that is changeless, that holds all together, that creates, dissolves, and recreates. That informing power of spirit is God.

—MAHATMA GANDHI

The true doctrine of omnipresence is that God reappears with all His parts in every moss and cobweb.

—RALPH WALDO EMERSON

There is no place to which we could flee from God which is outside God.

—PAUL TILLICH

God never leaves off making; as it is the property of fire to burn and of snow to chill, so it is of God to make.

—PHILO

You see many stars at night in the sky but find them not when the sun rises. . . . Because you behold not God in the days of your ignorance, say not there is no God.

—RAMAKRISHNA

GOD IS NOT A COSMIC BELLBOY FOR WHOM WE CAN PRESS A BUTTON TO GET THINGS DONE.

—HARRY EMERSON FOSDICK

When I saw others straining toward God, I did not understand it. . . . It is up to Him, after all, to have us, our part consists of almost solely in letting Him grasp us.

—RAINER MARIA RILKE

Chance is perhaps the pseudonym of God when He did not want to sign.

—ANATOLE FRANCE

When you knock, ask to see God—

none of the servants.

—HENRY DAVID THOREAU

The self-appointed spokesmen for God incline to shout; He, Himself, speaks only in whispers.

—MARTIN H. FISCHER

’TIS ONLY GOD MAY BE HAD FOR THE ASKING.

—JAMES RUSSELL LOWELL

And if you would know God be not therefore a solver of riddles. Rather look about you and you shall see Him playing with your children. And look into space; you shall see Him walking in the cloud, outstretching His arms in the lightning and descending in rain. You shall see Him smiling in flowers, then rising and waving His hands in trees.

—KAHLIL GIBRAN

My theology, briefly,

is that the universe was

dictated but not signed.

—CHRISTOPHER MORLEY

Life is a tapestry: We are the warp; angels, the weft; God, the weaver. Only the Weaver sees the whole design.

—EILEEN ELIAS FREEMAN

God can never be a definition.

He is more than even the

entirety of the dictionary.

—SCARLETT BENE

I believe the love of God may be taught not to seem like bears.

—EMILY DICKINSON

Every beauty which is seen here below by persons of perception resembles more than anything else that celestial source from which we all are come.

—MICHELANGELO

That deeply emotional conviction of the presence of a superior reasoning power, which is revealed in the incomprehensible universe, forms my idea of God.

—ALBERT EINSTEIN

THE UNIVERSE IS BUT ONE VAST SYMBOL OF GOD.

—THOMAS CARLYLE

Both sexes are created alike in the image of God—the Heavenly Mother and Father!

—ELIZABETH CADY STANTON

Every child has known God,

Not the God of names,

Nor the God of don'ts,

Nor the God who never does anything weird,

But the God who knows only four words

And keeps repeating them, saying:

"Come dance with me, come dance."

—HAFIZ

To love someone means to see him as God intended him.

—FYODOR DOSTOEVSKY

GOD'S GIFTS PUT MAN'S BEST DREAMS TO SHAME.

—ELIZABETH BARRETT BROWNING

All men were made by the same Great Spirit Chief.
They are all brothers. The Earth is the mother of all people,
and all people should have equal rights upon it.

—CHIEF JOSEPH, NEZ PERCE LEADER

The first peace, which is the most important, is that which comes within the souls of people when they realize their relationship, their oneness, with the universe and all its powers, and when they realize that at the center of the universe dwells Wakan-Taka (the Great Spirit), and that this center is really everywhere, it is within each of us.

—BLACK ELK, OGLALA SIOUX AND SPIRITUAL LEADER

Our God is the same God.

You may think now that you own Him as you wish to own our land; but you cannot. He is the God of all people, and His compassion is equal for all.

—CHIEF SEATTLE

The moment I have realized God sitting in the temple of every human body, the moment I stand in reverence before every human being and see God in him—that moment I am free from bondage, everything that binds vanishes, and I am free.

—SWAMI VIVEKANANDA

CONSCIENCE IS GOD PRESENT IN MAN.

—VICTOR HUGO

Were there no God, we would be in this glorious world with grateful hearts and no one to thank.

—CHRISTINA ROSSETTI

They say that God is everywhere, and yet we always think of Him as somewhat of a recluse.

—EMILY DICKINSON

God is an unutterable sigh,

planted in the depths of the soul.

—JEAN PAUL

I WOULD RATHER WALK WITH GOD IN THE DARK THAN GO ALONE IN THE LIGHT.

—MARY GARDINER BRAINARD

The more I know of astronomy, the more I believe in God.

—HEBER D. CURTIS

When you close your doors, and make darkness within, remember never to say that you are alone, for you are not alone; nay, God is within, and your genius is within.

—EPICTETUS

The great soul that sits on the throne of the universe is not, never was, and never will be, in a hurry.

—JOSIAH GILBERT HOLLAND

God is a sun, which, though but one, is sufficient to enlighten and vivify a whole world.

—MICHEL LE FAUCHEUR

You cannot believe in God

until you believe in yourself.

—SWAMI VIVEKANANDA

God is truth and light His shadow.

—PLATO

It is necessary that one should be convinced of God's existence, but not so necessary that one should prove it.

—IMMANUEL KANT

He who knoweth his own self, knoweth God.

—PROPHET MUHAMMAD

Our birth is but a sleep and a forgetting;

The soul that rises with us, our life's star,

Hath had elsewhere its setting,

And cometh from afar;

Not in entire forgetfulness,

And not in utter nakedness,

But trailing clouds of glory do we come

From God, who is our home.

—WILLIAM WORDSWORTH